CHAMPION SPORT

BIOGRAPHIES

MICHAEL JORDAN

CHAMPION SPORT

BIOGRAPHIES

MICHAEL JORDAN

MICHAEL BOUGHN

Warwick Publishing Inc.
Toronto Los Angeles
www.warwickgp.com

We acknowledge the financial support of the Government of Canada through the Book Publishing Industry Development Program for our publishing activities.

ISBN: 1-894020-51-0

Published by Warwick Publishing Inc.
162 John Street, Suite 300, Toronto, Ontario M5V 2E5
1300 North Alexandria Avenue, Los Angeles, California 90027

Distributed in the United States and Canada by Firefly Books Ltd.
3680 Victoria Park Avenue, Willowdale, Ontario M2H 3K1

Cover and layout design: Heidi Gemmill
Editorial Services: Joseph Romain
Cover Photo: Craig Robertson, Toronto Sun
Inside Photos: Page 58 Alex Urosevic, Toronto Sun
                      Page 59 Rene Johnston, Toronto Sun
                      Page 60 Michael Peake, Toronto Sun
                      Page 61 Craig Robertson, Toronto Sun
Printed and bound in Canada.

Table of Contents

Factsheet

Michael Jordan

Born Michael Jeffrey Jordan, February 17, 1963, Brooklyn, NY

Height: 6 feet, 6 inches (1.98 metres) Weight: 216 pounds (98 kg)

Attended the University of North Carolina

Favorite subject in school: math

Member of the NCAA Champion North Carolina Tar Heels, 1982

Selected after junior season by Chicago Bulls in first round (third pick overall) of 1984 NBA Draft

Career Highlights:

1984:	College Player of the Year; Olympic Gold Medallist
1985:	NBA Rookie of the Year
1986:	Most points scored in an NBA playoff (63)
1988:	Regular Season MVP
1991:	Regular Season MVP; Playoff MVP
1992:	Regular Season MVP; Playoff MVP; Olympic Gold Medallist
1993:	Playoff MVP
1996:	Scored 25,000th career point on 11/30; Playoff MVP; named one of the NBA's 50 greatest players
1997:	Playoff MVP

Chicago Bulls all-time leading scorer with 26,920 points; all-time assists leader with 4,729; all-time steals leader with 2,165 (1984–85 through 1992–93, and 1994–95 through 1996–97)

Introduction

In the baseball dream, they're more cheers of hope than cheers of expecting me to do good. They're cheering for me even though they don't know that I'll be good.

—Michael Jordan
Rebound: The Odyssey of Michael Jordan

It was a minor league ballpark in the southern United States sometime in April 1994. The sun had just gone down and the lights were on.

Off behind the third base-line seats, you could make out a grove of trees in the soft twilight where people were finishing up picnics of fried chicken and hush puppies before the game started. That night the home team, the Greenville Braves, a farm team for Atlanta, would be playing the Birmingham Barons, a farm team for the Chicago White Sox.

It was just another game in the Double A Southern League, small potatoes in the world of baseball. But it was one of those perfect times, a baseball time. The base paths stood out sharply in the cooling air, and the cicadas sent up a steady racket in the warm southern night.

But there was something funny about this game. For one thing, there were many more people there than you'd expect. Usually the Braves drew a crowd of about 1,000. Tonight over 8,000 fans packed the stands. There was a sense of anticipation, too, as if all those people were waiting for something special to happen.

As the Birmingham Barons took their positions on the field, the crowd hushed. Then, when the player with the number 45 on his uniform ran out to take his spot in right field, they went nuts. People stood up and cheered, shouted, waved, called out the player's name as if he were a superstar.

That's because he was. The man with 45 on his jersey playing right field for that small-time farm team in that small Southern town on that April night was probably the best basketball player alive. By the time he was 30 years old, he had been named National Basketball Association (NBA) Most Valuable Player three times, the last time only a few months before he took his place in right field.

He'd also been National Collegiate Athletic Association (NCAA) Player of the Year in 1983 and 1984, NBA Rookie of the Year in 1985, and NBA Defensive Player of the Year in 1988. Fans had voted him onto every NBA all-star team from 1985 to 1993, and he'd played with two gold medal–winning teams in the Olympics in 1984 and 1992. Some people thought he was one of the greatest American athletes of all time. He was certainly one of the very few to have a pair of shoes named after him — Air Jordans.

Player 45 was Michael Jordan, of course. And the fact that he was once again a rookie playing for a farm team in the lowly Class Double A Southern League was one of the great sports stories of the century. How did this mega-star, who was a millionaire many times over, a spokesman for major US corporations, a friend of movie stars and presidents, a hero to millions of kids, come to be standing under lights, brushing away mosquitoes, in a bush-league ball park in South Carolina?

It's not an easy question to answer. A lot of his fans were asking the same thing. Newspaper editorials and radio and TV broadcasters were calling on him to come back to Chicago and rejoin the Bulls, the basketball team he'd led to three straight NBA championship titles. There was a lot of pressure. But Michael Jordan was where he wanted to be, even if the rest of the world couldn't figure out why. And he planned to stay a while.

Michael Jordan exploded into basketball history in 1984, the year he went pro and was drafted by the Chicago Bulls. Many of those who followed college basketball in the NCAA already knew of this hardworking young athlete. In 1982, after his first season with the University of North Carolina Tar Heels, he'd been named Atlantic Coast Conference Rookie of the

Year. And in 1983, *Sporting News* had named him College Player of the Year. Still, the year he went pro, he was only the third-round draft pick, after Hakeem Olajuwon and Sam Bowie.

Basketball is a game for big men, and both the men chosen before Jordan in the draft were much bigger than he was. It's not just a question of height. Most players in the NBA stand around seven feet tall (2.13 metres) and weigh from 220 to 285 pounds (100 to 120 kilograms). Although basketball is supposed to be a "non-contact" sport, everybody knows it's not. Anyone driving down the lane in the middle of the court toward the basket has to run through a gauntlet of elbows and fast-moving bodies weighing hundreds of pounds. Jordan, at 6'6" (1.98m) and 200 pounds (91 kg), was small by comparison to most players in the NBA.

But what the Houston Rockets and the Portland Trailblazers didn't know when they passed over Michael Jordan in the first round of the draft was that he had a skill that made up for his size: He could fly.

It hadn't always been that way. Nobody in Michael Jordan's family was very big. But they all loved sports, and James Jordan, Michael's father, encouraged them to play hard, to give it everything they had. Basketball wasn't even Michael's first sport when he was a kid. He played Little League Baseball and dreamed of becoming a pitcher in the Majors. But when he got turned down for the varsity basketball team at Elmsley

Laney High School in Wilmington, North Carolina, suddenly nobody could hold him back.

Once he'd been told no, Michael Jordan pulled out all the stops. He worked out in the gym constantly. He lifted weights. His father even claimed he willed himself to grow. By his senior year at Laney, not only was he on the varsity team, he led them to a division championship, their first ever.

Michael Jordan never looked back. It was as if he realized for the first time what he could do. From Laney, he went to the University of North Carolina, where he played with Dean Smith's Tar Heels for three years, helping to lead them to their first NCAA championship. After that, it was the NBA and the Chicago Bulls where he broke record after record, constantly pushing himself to ever new accomplishments.

He has been named NBA Finals Most Valuable Player (MVP) six times and NBA MVP five times. He is the Bulls' all-time leading scorer, having scored over 29,000 career points. He was named to the NBA All-Defensive First Team nine times. He's played in twelve All-Star games, and been named All-Star MVP three times. He broke Kareem Abdul-Jabbar's NBA record by scoring double digits for 788 consecutive games. And eventually, he led the Bulls to six championships in eight years.

Along with success came fame. Michael Jordan became one of the most widely admired athletes in the world. Wherever he went he was mobbed by adoring fans. He couldn't go to the store or do business without finding himself surrounded by hundreds of people. All they wanted was to catch a glimpse of him, to be able to say they'd seen Michael Jordan.

And along with incredible fame came incredible wealth. Many major US corporations such as Nike, the sports-gear maker, and Cheerios, the breakfast cereal company, hired Michael Jordan to represent their products to the world. Almost overnight he became a multimillionaire. And every time his face went on another box of cereal or another billboard, he became even more famous.

There is a price that comes with all that fame. And it's a big price. Michael Jordan tells the story of being stopped at a red light in Chicago one day, waiting for the light to change. Suddenly someone was pounding on the window of his car. It was some guy who had left his own car idling, and was trying to get Michael Jordan to give him an autograph.

That kind of fame means that never again will you be able to do all the little things you take for granted. You won't be able to walk to the store. You won't be able to hang out in the park. You won't be able to jump into a game of pickup ball at the court down the street or at the local gym. Because any time you try to do those things, suddenly you'll find yourself mobbed by hundreds of people who want something from you.

Some people don't seem to mind that. But Michael Jordan isn't one of them. The one thing he has always cared about most — next to his family — is being able to play basketball. And suddenly, with all the fame, he found his ability to do that was more and more limited.

For Michael, the thrill of winning was great. But so was the thrill of learning, the thrill of pushing himself further than he thought he could, the thrill of mastering a sport. He called it "climbing the stairs." He had money. He had fame. But for the first time in his life, he couldn't do the thing he loved most anymore — he couldn't just play ball. Michael Jordan found himself, in some sense, trapped by his own success.

What do you do when you reach the height of success? When you break all the records? When everyone looks at you with awe? When the crowds close around and there's no place left to go?

In that situation, a lot of people would just keep playing till they retired. What other options could there be? For most people, none. But Michael Jordan is not most people. If there's one thing he possesses more then athletic skill and incredible determination, it's courage. When he came to that point in his life, he realized it was going to require all the courage he had to do what was right for him.

No one will ever know for sure what the guy out in right field was thinking that night as he waited under the lights for a hit to come his way. One thing was for sure, though. He was doing the thing he loved most. He was playing the game.

Chapter 1

Signs of Greatness

How can you say there isn't a plan for all of us?
— Michael Jordan
Vanity Fair, October 1998

In 1891, Dr. James Naismith, a Canadian from a small town in Ontario, was living in Springfield, Massachusetts, when he decided to nail two peach baskets to the balcony railings at opposite ends of the YMCA gym. The idea was to form two teams and have them try to throw a soccer ball through the baskets.

As the Athletic Director of the YMCA Training School, he was looking for a new sport that could be played inside during the cold Massachusetts winters. He had no idea that 100 years later the game that his friend wanted him to call Naismithball would become one of the most popular sports in the world.

Basketball has gone through many changes since Dr. Naismith first organized two teams and put them on the court. The first game took place in February 1892, between the Central and Armory Hill branches of the Springfield YMCA. It ended in a 2–2 tie. A month later they played again and Armory Hill won 1–0.

In those days, the game wasn't nearly as fast as it is today, mostly because the rules called for a center jump after every basket. Twenty points was a high score. The idea that one team, let alone one player, might score 40, 50, or even 60 points was unimaginable. So was the idea that black and white players might play on the same team.

The game had come a long way when Michael Jordan, not yet 10 years old, started playing in the 1960s. He didn't exactly play with peach baskets, but it wasn't far off. His first court was in the backyard of his parents' house in Wilmington, North Carolina. When Michael's older brother Larry got interested in the game, James Jordan, their father, decided to put up a basket on the back lawn. James Jordan loved sports and always encouraged his children to play hard.

Soon, the backyard was full of kids from all over the neighborhood. So many kids kept coming over that James Jordan decided to add another basket and make a full court. The Jordan boys called their new court "the Rack." Within a few days, they'd worn down all the grass between the two baskets and the earth became as hard as concrete.

Michael and his brother played a lot of one on one. Larry was taller and heavier than Michael at the time. He played hard, never giving his younger brother a break. That intense competition and the sting of constant defeat only drove Michael Jordan to play harder.

"Those backyard games really helped me become the player I am today," he said later. "Larry would never give me any slack, never took it easy on me. I learned a lot about being competitive from him." Competition was a part of every aspect of the brothers' lives. Michael and Larry's mother, Deloris Jordan, said that the only time they stopped competing was when they sat down to eat.

As Michael got older and began to grow bigger than Larry, the tables turned. "Michael started playing against Larry, who was only five feet seven inches [1.7 metres]," James Jordan said. "Back then, Larry was a little taller and much stronger than Michael who was still in grade school. Larry would beat Michael mercilessly. As Michael got older, he got bigger — and the games got much closer."

As Michael began to win the contests with Larry, he had to be prepared to fight for the right to do so, since Larry didn't much care to lose to his younger brother.

Basketball wasn't Michael's only sport. In fact, in his school years his favorite sport was baseball. In junior high school, when he was 12 years old, he pitched a two-hitter. That year he led the Wilmington team to within one game of making the Little League World Series. He was named the Most Valuable Player in the Babe Ruth League when his team won the state championship. He batted .500 and hit five home runs in seven games.

Even as he started attending E. A. Laney High School in Wilmington, Michael was still excelling at many different sports. He was five feet ten inches tall (1.78 metres) by then. He quarterbacked the junior varsity football team. He ran track.

But when he tried out for the varsity basketball team, he suffered his first real setback. Much to his surprise, he didn't make the team.

Only the school's best athletes made it to the varsity teams. Michael was embarrassed and hurt that he didn't qualify. What he didn't know then was that the coach of the varsity basketball team had held him back on purpose. Michael was already showing signs of being such a good player that the coach felt letting him play on the varsity team when he was only in his second year of high school would go to his head. It would be better for Michael's development, the coach felt, if he played with the junior varsity team and developed his skills.

The coach's plan worked. Even though Michael felt hurt, all the competitiveness he'd learned in his relationship with Larry came to his rescue. Rather than getting down on himself or the coach, he decided that he would do whatever it took to make the varsity team. Nothing, he decided, would stop him.

Instead of feeling sorry for himself, Michael started playing basketball every minute he could. He played with the junior varsity team, and every day, before and after school, he worked out in the gym. That summer he played every day. He did drill after drill to perfect his basketball skills.

As strange as it sounds, he also worked on growing. James Jordan once came into Michael's bedroom that year and found him hanging from the chin-up bar. "What are you doing?" he asked.

Michael told him he was stretching himself. James Jordan used to tell people that Michael literally willed himself to grow. That's the kind of determination he had. By the fall, he'd added five inches (12 centimetres) to his height from the previous year. Now he was six feet three inches tall (1.9 m). He had also developed all his basketball skills.

Michael didn't just play sports in high school. He was a good student, and he participated in various other activities. He was in the Spanish Club and the Pep Club. He played trumpet in the band for a while. Most of his classmates at Laney thought of him as outgoing and easy to get along with. He had friends in many different groups in the school.

The one thing he was nervous about was girls. He was so uncomfortable with girls that he thought he'd grow up to be a bachelor. That's why he took Home Economics. He learned how to hem clothes and cut out patterns. He even made his own shirt and baked cakes and bread that he took home to his family.

The fall of 1979, when Michael started his third year at Laney, he easily made the varsity basketball team. He could run, jump, and handle the ball better than anyone else in Laney High School. Even so, his first year on the team didn't start well. Michael seemed to completely lose control when he got on the court. He made wild shots and kept turning the ball over to the other team. He played so badly he was in danger of being replaced. He was devastated.

Then, suddenly, everything came together for him. It was during a holiday basketball tournament at Christmas. Laney made the finals and was scheduled to play against their archrivals, New Hanover High. New Hanover dominated most of the game, though Laney managed to keep up.

In the fourth quarter, Laney was trailing when, suddenly, Michael Jordan turned into a powerhouse. All of the hard work, all of the training seemed to fall into place. He began to show the incredible skill that would take him to the pros. He flew through the air, spun around, and dunked the ball. He intercepted passes, and stole the ball from opposing players. He scored over and over. But New Hanover still managed to keep up.

With only seconds left to play, Laney trailed New Hanover by one point. Michael Jordan came up with the ball, leaped into the air, and shot from 15 feet (4.57m) out. The crowd watched silently as the ball sailed through the air. When it swished through the net, they exploded with excitement. Michael Jordan had not only scored the game-winning point, he had scored all of Laney's last 15 points. It was a glimpse into the future. For the first time, Michael Jordan had a glimmer of what he was capable of.

For the rest of the year, Michael was a different player. His awkwardness and wildness disappeared. Everything gelled for him. He became the backbone of the Laney team.

At the end of his junior year in high school, Michael Jordan was not known outside of North Carolina. He wasn't even among the 300 top players college scouts listed as the most promising high school players in the US at the end of the 1980 season. In North Carolina, however, he was beginning to get a reputation. Dean Smith, the coach of the University of North Carolina (UNC) Tar Heels, heard about this unknown player from Wilmington and invited him to attend his sportscamp so he could get a look at him. Michael Jordan was 17 years old. The world was about to change for him.

Every summer, Dean Smith held his basketball camp at UNC. It was a way for him and his assistant coaches to scout the various players coming up through the high schools in North Carolina and build relationships with them. In this way, he managed to lock up most of the good high school players in North Carolina for his team.

Michael went to the camp with his friend Harvey Leroy Smith. They roomed with two other players, Buzz Peterson, who would become Michael's good friend, and Randy Shepherd. Peterson was already a well-known high school athlete in the state. Going into the camp, he and another player, Lynwood Robinson, were the two players the UNC scouts were most interested in recruiting for the university. By the end of the camp, however, Michael Jordan was at the top of their list.

Out of the 400 kids who came to the camp, Michael stood out as far and away the best. His ability and his drive deeply impressed the UNC coaches. According to Roy Williams, later the head coach at University of Kansas, the UNC coaches had decided that if they were allowed only one player in the country, Michael would be it. They wanted to try and keep him a secret from other schools that might be able to offer him a better deal than UNC could.

But by the end of Michael's stay at the camp, word had gotten out about this tremendous, unknown player from Wilmington. As a result, he got invited to the best basketball camp in the United States — the 5-Star Camp.

The 5-Star Camp was in Pittsburgh. The very best high school players from across the country were there. Michael and his friend from Dean Smith's camp, Leroy Smith, went there together.

Michael was both scared and excited to be at the camp. College scouts from all over the US went to the 5-Star Camp, which was an intensive three-week basketball session. Based on what they saw there, many of the high school students would be offered scholarships to the best athletic programs in the country. Seventeen high school All-Americans would be selected at the camp. Some of them would receive up to 100 recruitment letters from colleges and universities.

Hardly anybody there had ever heard of this young player from Wilmington when the camp started. But that didn't last for long. It was as if playing against other very good players only inspired Michael to play that much harder. He excelled. Howie Garfinkle, who ran the camp, thought Michael was not only quicker and could jump higher than anyone else, he was also in control. Most kids his age with his degree of physical ability were all over the map. But Michael wasn't. This was where all those hours of drill, drill, and more drill in the high school gym and the backyard court really began to pay off.

When the camp ended, Michael was asked to stay another week. The second week, his friend Buzz Peterson came to the camp. They played together a lot that second week, and got quite close. By the end of the week, Michael had suggested to Peterson that they go to UNC together. At the 5-Star Camp, Michael began to realize for the first time how great his abilities actually were. And how far they might take him.

"It was the turning point in my life," he says.

By the fall of 1980, when he was entering his senior year of high school, Michael had grown another two inches (five cm). He stood now at six feet five inches (1.95 m). He spent every spare minute in the school gym. He was there when the sun came up. He was there when the sun went down. When the school year started, he played on both the varsity and the junior varsity teams at Laney so he could get more court time. And when he wasn't playing in the gym, he was playing in the backyard.

Michael became so driven to perfect his skills at basketball that he even started cutting some of his classes. When the principal found out, he suspended Michael from school.

Michael's parents weren't very happy to hear that he had been skipping school. As much as they encouraged him in his pursuit of excellence on the basketball court, they also knew that the most important thing he could do for himself was to get a good education. His father sat him down and pointed out to him that without good grades he'd never get into university. And that would be the end of his basketball career.

Realizing his father was right, Michael stopped cutting classes and began to seriously apply himself to his schoolwork. Soon his grades were back up. That fall, Michael publicly announced that he would be going to the University of North Carolina the following year.

Many different schools were trying to attract Michael now that they realized what a great basketball player he was. Every day he would come home to find more letters from colleges and universities offering him scholarships if he would only come play for them. He had written to UCLA, but got no answer from them. In the meantime, Dean Smith and some of his assistant coaches had been nurturing a relationship with Michael and his family. Finally, at the beginning of his senior year at Laney, Michael decided that he'd go to the University of North Carolina.

But he didn't ease up on his training schedule. Because he pushed himself so hard, Michael's skills on the court just kept improving with every game. In his last high school basketball season he averaged 23 points per game. One by one, every Laney scoring record fell to his determined playing. To top it all off, Michael led the Laney team to its first conference championship. Now, it seemed the world lay before him. All he had to do was go out and seize hold of it.

Chapter 2

Pushing the Envelope

Being competitive is really a way to constantly challenge myself, and I like to challenge myself in every aspect of my life. I believe there is always room for improvement.

— Michael Jordan
Michael Jordan

A lot of people thought Michael Jordan had made the wrong decision when he chose the University of North Carolina. Not that the Tar Heels weren't a great team. They were top ranked in the NCAA. But Dean Smith tightly controlled the players on his team. He had very definite ideas about how the game should be played, and those ideas didn't include relying on hotshot players. Of all the people trying to recruit Michael Jordan, Dean Smith was the only one who didn't offer him a spot on the starting lineup. Michael would have to earn it.

Dean Smith was known as someone who demanded discipline from all his players. His system involved teamwork, a tight defense, and a controlled offense known as the Four Corners. The Four Corners offense involved stationing players in a four-cornered pattern in front of the net. They were supposed to pass the ball around the box until someone had a good shot. It was a system that relied not on stars or individual excellence, but on the ability of a group of players to work together.

Over the years, the Tar Heels had been a top-ranked NCAA team. They'd been in the NCAA five times under Dean Smith's leadership, but they'd never won a championship. The year before Michael Jordan joined the team, they'd lost the championship to University of Indiana. Some people blamed Smith's system, especially his Four Corners offense. It definitely meant that Michael Jordan wouldn't be getting as much time on the court as he would if he'd chosen to go to some other school.

Everybody knows it's one thing being a big fish in a small pond, and a whole different thing when the pond suddenly gets a lot bigger. That's what Michael Jordan was feeling when he started attending the University of North Carolina in the fall of 1981. It's always a difficult adjustment. High schools are small places. A popular student like Michael Jordan can know almost everybody. Universities are much larger. When you're starting out you feel lost in the crowd of strange faces rushing between classes. High school classes seem hard, too, until you get to university and realize what hard really is.

Michael Jordan had to go through all those changes that are normal for freshmen. On top of them, he also had to deal with the fact that he was suddenly playing basketball with people who were far better than anyone he'd ever played with before. People had been telling him he was a good basketball player. Now he'd find out how good.

One day Michael Jordan wandered over to the gym. Official practice hadn't started yet, but he was looking for a pickup game, the kind of action he loved best. Sure enough, he found a group of guys playing. It wasn't your ordinary pickup game, though. Not only were two All-Americans in the game — James Worthy and Sam Perkins — but so were Mitch Kupchak and Al Wood. They were UNC alumni who had been drafted into the NBA and were still hanging around campus before the pro season started. This was a pickup game like Michael Jordan had never seen before.

When the guys on the court saw the new freshman standing on the sidelines, they invited him to join the game. Needless to say Michael was a little nervous. Because of that he played a pretty conservative game. As the end of the game approached, his team was losing by one point. Suddenly, he was thrown the ball. Without thinking, he drove to the basket and leaped to make his shot. Nobody thought he could do it since he was guarded by Al Wood and seven-foot (2.13 m) Geoff Compton.

As his teammates watched, he made what would become a classic Michael Jordan move. Somehow he managed to twist and slip through the guards, moving the ball from hand to hand, then dunking it to score the winning point. The other players were astonished. They clapped him on the back and congratulated him. He knew then that he was with his peers.

As good as he was, Michael Jordan was not guaranteed a spot in the Tar Heels' starting lineup. In the history of Dean Smith's coaching at UNC, only three freshmen had ever been allowed to start for the Tar Heels. Few people expected that Michael Jordan would. Even Michael had his doubts when he found out at the beginning of official practice that there was only one open spot in the lineup. He had certain advantages, though, that the players he was competing against didn't have.

Probably the most important advantage was that the Laney High School basketball teams had used the same offense as the Tar Heels. Because of that, Michael was able to fit effortlessly into the plays Coach Smith called for. Coach Smith noticed that no one was able to guard Michael Jordan. He was impressed with his new player, even if he was a freshman. Much to many people's surprise, Michael made the starting lineup against Kansas.

And he did well, too, although he had a bit of a shaky start. Feeling the pressure, he was nervous when he went out on the court. He missed his first shot. But he came back quickly. By the end of the game, he had scored 12 points in a 74–67 UNC win. He played well all season, and the Tar Heels finished with a 24–2 record. They went on to win the Atlantic conference championship and the conference tournament.

The 1982 NCAA playoffs were grueling. There was more than once when it looked like UNC might not make the finals. They barely won against James Madison University, 52–50, and pulled out a couple of equally close games against Alabama and Houston.

They finally overcame those obstacles, however, and made the finals. They would be playing against Georgetown University, whose freshman center, Patrick Ewing, was thought by some to be an even better player than Michael Jordan.

The two teams were evenly matched and they fought a tough game with each other. The lead seesawed back and forth between them. With only three minutes left to play, the Tar Heels were ahead 59–58. They struggled to hold onto their lead, but Patrick Ewing and Eric Floyd both scored for Georgetown, giving them a three-point lead. The Tar Heels managed to score again, making it 62–61 for Georgetown. There were only 32 seconds left in the game, and Dean Smith called a time out.

Georgetown was covering UNC's All-Americans, Worthy and Perkins, very closely, making it hard for them to get shots. But because Michael Jordan was a freshman, they were leaving him more room. It was a long shot, but Dean Smith, knowing they had only one chance to win, decided the ball should go to Michael.

Jimmy Black threw the ball in for UNC, and he and Jordan passed it back and forth till Black was challenged for the ball. He snapped it to Matt Doherty. The Georgetown defense started to form under the basket. Doherty threw the ball back to Black, who faked out the Georgetown defense, then passed the ball to Michael Jordan. He was wide open, 17 feet (5m) out from the net.

Michael's friend Buzz Peterson remembers thinking that Michael wouldn't take the shot because he was too far out. "There was so much pressure on him. I thought he would go back inside to James Worthy. But he was wide open and took the shot."

And what a shot it was. Michael jumped into the air, hung there, then flipped the ball toward the basket. It arched gracefully through the air, the crowd watching it in silence. Finally it snapped through the basket. The Tar Heels pulled in front 63–62. Georgetown didn't have time to score again. UNC won the NCAA championship for the first time, and millions of people had seen Michael make what became known as "the shot." Michael Jordan was suddenly one of the best-known college athletes in the United States.

Despite his new fame, it was still practice, practice, and more practice for Michael Jordan. He practically lived in the gym that summer after the NCAA win.

The following year, the Tar Heels played without James Worthy, who had gone on to the NBA, and they felt the loss. Even Michael Jordan playing his heart out couldn't make up for the loss of Worthy, who was not only a great player, but an important leader. Michael and Sam Perkins were called on to take over the role of team leaders. Michael pushed everyone hard, and no one harder than himself.

"He got to a point in his sophomore year," Buzz Peterson said, "when his confidence was really rolling and he'd tease the guys. He dunked on everybody."

Some people thought Michael Jordan was a show-off, but as Peterson said, "It takes a lot of cockiness to be a great player. When you step onto the court, you've got to say, 'I'm the best player out there.' Michael has always been that type of player and that's what he's always said."

The Tar Heels won the ACC championship again in 1983, but failed to make the NCAA finals. Nevertheless, Michael Jordan had a good enough year that *Sporting News* named him the College Player of the Year. He had averaged 20 points and 5.5 rebounds per game. The *Sporting News* described a Jordan that the entire country was soon to become familiar with: "He soars through the air, he rebounds, he scores, he guards two men at once. He vacuums up loose balls. He makes steals. Most important, he makes late plays that win games. Call it what you may, court sense or court presence. He has it."

That summer Michael was invited to join the US team playing in the Pan-American Games. The games were in Venezuela in 1983, which meant that Michael got to travel outside the country for the first time in his life. It was an eye-opening experience for him. He loved being in a different culture. It really made him aware of how big the world is.

One result of those games was that the US won a gold medal in basketball. Another result was that Michael Jordan decided he would major in cultural geography at UNC. That meant he would be studying other cultures and the ways their development had been influenced by geographical factors.

When Michael Jordan started his third year at UNC, he was one of the best-known university basketball players in the world. Acknowledging Michael's abilities as a team leader, Coach Smith gave him permission to use his own judgement on the court. For the first time, he was to be permitted to break out of the tight discipline of the Four Corner offense if he felt he could make a shot.

All the extra responsibilities meant extra stress for Michael, and it showed in his game. He started off poorly, missing shots. His game average went into the dumps. Many people started to wonder if they had misjudged him. Perhaps he wasn't the superstar they'd thought him to be.

That was the kind of pressure Michael always found himself under now. Having played so well, fans now expected him to play that way all the time. He was no longer just another basketball player. He was "Michael Jordan, superstar," and the minute he stumbled or showed some flaw, the critics were all over him like flies on honey.

By January, though, he had found his game again. Suddenly he was everywhere, making shots, blocking shots, stealing the ball, rebounding, and doing it all with more and more flash. He just kept getting better and better, and by the time the Tar Heels won the ACC championship and tournament, they were ranked Number 1 in the US. They beat the Temple University team with no problem.

But when they met Indiana, they couldn't figure out how to get past Bobby Knight's team. They lost the semi-final game 72–68 and failed to make the NCAA finals again.

That was the end of Michael Jordan's third year playing college basketball. Even though the Tar Heels were never able to duplicate their NCAA championship win, they played well and Michael Jordan continued to win Most Valuable Player awards.

But it was becoming obvious to Michael that he had accomplished just about everything he could playing college ball. There was little left for him to learn at that level of play.

The Tar Heels had won one NCAA championship and two ACC championships. Michael had won just about every award he could, and he had learned everything Dean Smith had to teach him. If he was to continue to grow as a player, he needed new challenges. And that meant the National Basketball Association.

Everybody agreed Michael Jordan was ready for the NBA. Even Coach Smith felt that Michael should seriously consider making the move. Smith's main concern was injuries. So far Michael had escaped any serious injuries. But if he played another year of college ball, there was no telling what might happen. If he hurt himself badly, he might never get to play pro basketball.

There was also the question of money. As one of the two or three top-ranked college players, Michael could make some serious money if he moved to the NBA. After years of scraping by and, more important, watching his parents scrape by, Michael was ready for that.

Some people opposed the move. They felt that Michael Jordan owed it to UNC and the Tar Heels to lead them to another NCAA championship. Those voices didn't bother Michael much. As he said later, "I have to do what's best for me. If I owe anyone, it's my parents, who have put up with me for 20 years."

But his parents, and especially his mother, were among those who didn't want him to go pro. Deloris Jordan continued to feel that no matter how good a basketball player Michael was, there was no substitute for a good education.

"No matter where you go," she told him, "or how much money you make, you'll always have your education. They can take your clothes. They can take your shoes. But they can't take what's in your head."

While Michael Jordan pondered these issues, trying to decide what to do, he was presented with yet another honor. He was asked to try out for the US Olympic Basketball team.

In 1984, only amateur athletes were allowed into the Olympics, unlike today. To be asked to try out was a tremendous honor. Being selected was an even greater one. But before he could go on to play for the United States, he had to decide what to do about his career.

Michael Jordan agonized right down to the wire. Even though Dean Smith was encouraging him to go pro, Michael still wasn't sure it was the right thing to do. He called a press conference for May 5, 1984, the absolute last minute he had to declare himself eligible for the NBA Draft. According to his roommate Buzz Peterson, the night before, Michael was still going back and forth in his mind, weighing the pros and cons.

Finally in the morning, just before the press conference, he knew what he had to do. "Money plays a big part in our lives," he told the assembled reporters. "But who knows? I may not be around next year. I think it's better to start now."

Typically, however, Michael Jordan wanted to make it clear that although money was important, it wasn't everything. "But this wasn't solely a financial decision," he went on. "Here was a chance to move to a higher level."

There was one more thing to take care of, however. Although his mother understood and supported his decision, she was still deeply concerned that he finish his education. He promised her that he would return to school the next two summers and finish his degree. It's a mark of Michael Jordan's integrity that even after he went on to the NBA and became a multimillionaire and hero to millions, he kept his word to his mother. He was awarded his Bachelor of Arts degree in 1986.

Chapter 3

Learning the Ropes

All I wanted to do was win, but you hear this stuff about "Michael carrying too much of the load" and whether that's good for the team.

— Michael Jordan
Jordan: The Man, His Words, His Life

Every year, representatives from the National Basketball Association teams meet to recruit top college athletes who have decided to become professionals. The first draft choices go to the teams with the worst records. When the NBA team reps met for the annual college draft in 1984, Michael Jordan was considered among the top prospects.

But he wasn't necessarily Number 1. Most of the teams with early picks were looking for tall men, and at 6'6" (1.98 m), Michael Jordan wasn't particularly tall by NBA standards. Hakeem Olajuwon was 6'10" (2.08 m). He was the choice of the Houston Rockets. After Houston came the Portland Trailblazers. They picked 7'1" (2.16 m) Sam Bowie.

It wasn't until the Chicago Bulls, who had the third-round pick, made their choice that Michael Jordan finally heard his name called out.

In 1984, the Bulls were one of the worst franchises in the NBA. The team had been founded in 1966. Over the years they'd been in some playoffs, and in 1972 they'd even won the Central Division championship. But they'd never gone as far as the NBA finals. And recently, their record had been terrible. The year before they selected Michael Jordan, they'd finished next to last, with a mere 27 wins to 55 losses.

Everyone agreed that the team lacked leadership on the court. The Bulls management was hoping that if they could pick up Michael Jordan in the draft, they could change that.

Even so, Michael Jordan wouldn't have been their first choice if there had been another center available. They knew he was a good player, but he was a guard. Like Portland and Houston, they thought at the time that a center would have been a better choice.

But then Chicago wasn't Michael Jordan's first choice either. Personally, he would have preferred to play for the Philadelphia 76ers. As it turned out though, it was a match made, as they say, in heaven.

Before Michael Jordan could sign with the Bulls, however, he had some other business to take care of. The Olympics were coming up in 1984. In those days, in order to play in the Olympics, an athlete had to be an amateur. That meant that Michael Jordan had to put off signing with the Bulls until after he played in the Olympic games, which were in Los Angeles that year. Bobby Knight, the Olympic team's coach, named Michael Jordan co-captain of a team that included Patrick Ewing, Sam Perkins, and Chris Mullin.

Michael practiced all summer with the Olympians. They also played a series of exhibition games with NBA teams in order to prepare. The Olympians took eight games in a row from the pros, including the rough and tumble final game when the NBA players tried to physically bully their way to victory.

The US Olympic basketball team had the right stuff. They took games from China, Canada, Uruguay, and then beat Spain in the finals. In the end, they took all eight of their games and won the Olympic gold medal.

Michael Jordan was the undisputed, dynamic leader of the team. For the first time, the rest of world became aware of this extraordinary player. Asked to comment on the US team, Fernando Martin of the Spanish team replied, "Michael Jordan. Jump, jump, jump. Very quick. Very fast, very, very good. Jump, jump, jump!" In the end, Michael had scored an average of 17 points per game.

It was a stirring moment for everyone at the medal presentation ceremony. Michael Jordan stood with tears in his eyes. Searching the crowd, he found his mother,

Deloris. After the ceremony, he sought her out, took the medal off his own neck, and hung it around hers.

As soon as the Olympic games were over, Michael signed a seven-year contract with the Bulls for six million dollars. The contract also contained one extraordinary clause. NBA teams usually do not let their players join in pickup games because they worry about unnecessary injuries. Michael Jordan insisted that his contract allow him to play pickup games, and the Bulls agreed. It showed how badly they wanted him on their team.

It also showed Michael Jordan's desire, even as he entered the world of professional sports, to keep playing the game he grew up with. There was no way even a six-million-dollar paycheck was going to keep him from doing what he loved most, including playing basketball with his brother Larry.

As Michael began playing with the Bulls, he found professional basketball was a much different game than college ball. It was much quicker and there was much more room for individual abilities to blossom. Michael had learned valuable lessons about teamwork and discipline from Dean Smith. But within the rigorous structure of Smith's game, he had had to keep some of his own abilities under wraps. Suddenly he found himself in a situation where he could open up.

And that's just what he did. In his first exhibition

game, he scored 22 points while being guarded by Milwaukee's Sidney Moncrief, the NBA Defensive Player of the Year.

Meanwhile, other things were starting to change in Michael's life. His fame was spreading like wildfire through the NBA. Along with the fame came numerous offers to appear in advertisements. His agent, David Faulk, had worked out a deal with the Nike company to name a pair of sneakers after his client.

At first, Nike wanted to call the shoes "Prime Time." But Faulk thought that sounded too much like a TV show. After some thinking, he came up with the name "Air Jordan." He thought that would connect the air pockets built into the shoe's soles with Michael's incredible jumping ability. Within two years, Nike had sold $130 million worth of Air Jordan shoes. Some people began calling Michael Jordan the greatest shoe salesman in history.

There's a story that before the first game of the 1984–85 season, Coach Dean Smith came up from North Carolina to visit Michael in the Bulls' dressing room. There he presented Michael with a pair of Tar Heel shorts. Ever since that night, Michael Jordan has worn the Tar Heel shorts under his Bulls shorts for luck.

Michael Jordan adjusted quickly to the NBA and was soon the leading Bulls scorer in every game. He rapidly became a national sensation. His astonishing athletic prowess, his ability to seemingly hang in the air while the players around him fell to the ground, quickly caught the imagination of the public. Wherever the Bulls were playing, thousands of fans turned out just to see Michael Jordan.

Overnight, Michael's life had changed utterly, and not all for the better. Suddenly he found he couldn't go out to a restaurant without being mobbed by fans. He couldn't go to the store to buy a pair of shoes without being trapped in the store by crowds of adoring people. He no longer could do the ordinary everyday things the rest of us take for granted. It was a struggle for him to get used to that, and in some ways he never has.

He played well, though, and in mid-season was excited to be named for the first time to the NBA All-Star team. The game, however, didn't turn out the way he had hoped. Although he played for 22 minutes, he took only nine shots, and missed seven of those. The ball always seemed to be going to someone else, even when he was in the clear. No one on his own team helped him out when he did get the ball. When the game was over, he was extremely disappointed with his performance. He couldn't figure out what had happened.

He soon found out, however. It seems he had been the subject of a plot by other players. Some of them felt that Michael was a glory hound. Organized by Isiah Thomas of the Detroit Pistons, they had decided to teach the rookie a lesson by keeping the ball away from him.

When Michael found out about the plan, he was embarrassed and angry. He decided to pay Thomas back on the court. When the Bulls next played the Pistons, Michael soared, drove the ball down court, jumped, and generally humiliated the Pistons. He scored 49 points in one game, leading the Bulls to a 139–126 victory.

There were other things going on in Michael Jordan's life apart from basketball. In 1985, his eye was caught by one of the secretaries at an advertising agency he worked with. He found out her name was Juanita Vanoy. It took him some courage, but finally he asked her out. She was a former model and really didn't care much for basketball, which suited Michael just fine. It meant she related to him as a person, not as a superstar. They dated a lot, and soon were engaged to be married.

The Bulls were making changes, too. They realized that no matter how good Michael Jordan was, they needed to strengthen the team as a whole if they wanted to win championships. They acquired forward Charles Oakley. The season looked like it would shape up well. Then disaster struck.

On October 29, 1985, the Bulls were playing the Oakland Golden State Warriors. In the second period Michael Jordan was moving on the basket when suddenly he went down. His teammates gathered around to help him up, but he couldn't walk by himself. He had to be assisted into the locker room.

The doctor looked at Michael's foot and said he had a sprained ankle. It didn't get any better, though, and a week later the doctor decided to do some more tests. A CAT scan of Michael's ankle revealed a small break in one of the bones. His foot was put in a cast.

It was certainly bad news for the Bulls. They began losing games regularly. At first, Michael came to the games and sat on the sidelines. But after a while he decided that his presence might be hurting the team, so he stopped coming. It didn't make much difference for the Bulls, but it did for Michael. He went back to UNC and finished his university degree, just as he had promised his mother he would.

Michael Jordan rejoined the Bulls lineup on March 15, 1986, after being out for 64 games. As soon as he was back with the team, they began winning games. The Bulls' owner, Jerry Reinsdorf, wanted Michael to take it easy and work his way back into the game slowly. He was worried that Michael might re-injure his ankle if he tried to do too much too quickly. Michael Jordan, however, was tired of sitting around. He was ready to play basketball again. After several long arguments with Reinsdorf, Michael Jordan got his way. The Bulls managed to make the last spot in the playoffs. This year they would be going up against the Boston Celtics.

Michael's performance in the playoffs was outstanding. In the first game against Boston, the Celtics double teamed him the whole game. But even with two players covering him, he still managed to score 49 points. It wasn't enough, though, and the Bulls lost 123–104.

In the second game Michael pulled out all the stops, scoring an astounding 63 points. It was the first time in playoff history anyone had scored that many points in one game. The Celtics still won the game, but even they could talk about nothing else but Michael Jordan's performance.

"I think he's God disguised as Michael Jordan," Larry Bird said after the game.

But no matter how well Michael Jordan played, he couldn't win it by himself. The Celtics took the next game in Chicago as well, sweeping the series once again.

It was a great disappointment for Michael Jordan. He had won every prize he'd ever set out to get except for one — an NBA championship. It was beginning to seem like he'd never get one.

On top of that disappointment came another. Increasingly he found himself the subject of criticism by sports writers and some basketball fans. They said that he wasn't a team player, that he was a glory hound. They started calling the Bulls "Team Jordan" or "Michael and the Jordanaires."

That criticism hurt. Michael Jordan knew there was an element of truth to it. The Bulls were far too reliant on his scoring abilities. But he didn't want it to be that way. He took no pleasure in it. He'd been trained as a team player at UNC, and wanted nothing more than to have a winning team to play with.

The problem was that even with the acquisition of Charles Oakley, the Bulls still did not have the depth of talent necessary to win championships. So Michael found himself having to choose between being more of a team player but losing games, or being called names but winning games. He preferred to win the games.

The criticism only got louder during the 1986–87 season. It was Michael's third season in the NBA and he just kept getting better and better as a player. He was once again elected to the All-Star team. This time he won a new honor. For the first time he won the slam dunk title at the All-Star game. He split the $12,000 prize up among his teammates.

But none of that was enough for his critics. They demanded nothing less than an NBA championship, and if Chicago didn't win it, they knew who to blame.

Chicago made the playoffs again in 1987, once again playing against Boston. And in a repeat perfor- mance, Boston swept the series in three games. The Bulls were demoralized. The voices of the critics of Michael Jordan rose in a shrill clamor, blaming him for not being a team player.

Chapter 4

Climbing the Mountain

I wanted to show that I can play defense and that I don't shoot as much as Larry Bird would say.

— Michael Jordan
Michael Jordan

The Bulls had been doing well, but not well enough to win championships. Aside from Charles Oakley and John Paxson, Michael Jordan was the only consistent scorer. Oakley's points were all on rebounds, and Paxson, while he was good from outside, hadn't yet created his own shot.

The Bulls needed more aggressive scorers who could set up plays and shoot from outside. They got them in the 1987 draft when they picked up forwards Scottie Pippen and Horace Grant, setting the stage for the development of one of the all-time great basketball teams.

Suddenly, Michael Jordan had people to work with. There's a word, "synergy", which refers to what happens when the combined effect of the parts is much more powerful than the sum of individual effects.

That's what happened to the Bulls. With his new teammates, Michael Jordan could suddenly stretch his wings as a playmaker. And it turned out he was a good one, something he had known all along, but never been able to prove. It was clear to many people that things were changing for the Bulls.

After getting off to a 7–1 start, the Bulls finished the first half of the season at 27–18. They ended the regular season tied for second place in the Central Division. They were clearly a different team this season and many people were predicting that they might go all the way to the NBA championship they wanted so badly.

They played Cleveland in the first round of the playoffs, winning the first two games. Michael Jordan scored 50 points in the first game and 55 in the second. But he couldn't do it alone. Pippen and Grant weren't playing to their potential, and the Bulls lost the next two games. In the last game, Pippen and Grant warmed up and found their groove, and the Bulls won the series, advancing to play the Detroit Pistons.

But the Pistons were ready for them. They'd been studying the Bulls' game, and had developed a special defense called "the Jordan rules." The Jordan rules were a way of shutting down Michael Jordan by double, triple, and even quadruple teaming him.

The Pistons had a reputation as one of the roughest teams in the NBA, and they never hesitated to simply knock Michael down if he did manage to get the ball. The Jordan rules worked well, and the Pistons beat the Bulls in five games.

It wasn't a bad season for Michael Jordan. He averaged 35 points a game, leading the league. But his real goal now was an NBA championship. Only that achievement would prove he was the equal of Magic Johnson and Larry Bird, both of whom had won championships with their teams.

Over the next two years, between 1988 and 1990, the Bulls made further key changes to their team and staff. They knew they were on the right track, but were still looking for the magic combination that would put it all together. They got Bill Cartwright at center, and even more important, replaced Coach Doug Collins with Phil Jackson. Jackson had played in the NBA for 13 years and not only knew the game, but had a special connection with the players.

Scottie Pippen and Horace Grant just kept getting better and better, too. Before long, everyone in the starting lineup was scoring in the double digits. There was much less reliance on Michael Jordan to carry the game. The Bulls were shaping up to be a powerhouse team. Everyone was working together.

But they weren't quite there yet. In both the 1988–89 season and the 1989–90 season the Bulls ran up against the Detroit Pistons and got stopped in their tracks. Even though the Bulls no longer depended almost totally on Michael Jordan to carry the game for them, he was still a very important part of their team. Detroit's Jordan rules defense continued to shut him down, and when he was shut down, so were the Bulls. In the 1990 playoffs, though, the Bulls fought the Pistons down to the wire, taking the series the full seven games. It was a sign that Detroit's days as NBA champion were numbered.

In 1989, Michael Jordan had some other good things happen in his life. He and his wife, Juanita, had their first child, a son they named Jeffrey. It was the beginning of their family, and they were both extremely happy. Michael Jordan very much loved being a father. The world looked good to him. It was about to get better.

At the beginning of the 1990–91 series, everyone agreed that the Bulls defense was much better than it had been. In the season opener, they went up against their old enemy, the Pistons. For the first time, they out-played them on both defense and offense. Chicago had become such a strong team that the Jordan rules simply didn't work any more. The Bulls rolled over the Pistons 98–86. Many people saw the game as a preview of what was to come in the playoffs.

The signs of greatness were all there. Phil Jackson's coaching was pushing the team to greater and greater heights. In December 1990, the Bulls set a regulation-game record when they scored 155 points against the Phoenix Suns. But the changes were especially appar-ent in the Bulls' final record for the season. They won 61 games and lost only 21. It was the second-best record in the league, and the best ever for the Bulls.

They breezed through the playoffs. First they beat the New York Knicks in three games, then went through Philadelphia in five. When they met the Pistons again, they completely turned the tables on them, stomping them in four straight games. Clearly, things had changed for the Bulls.

The NBA finals matched the Bulls against the Los Angeles Lakers. Everyone was pitching the series as a showdown between LA's Magic Johnson and Chicago's Michael Jordan.

Michael Jordan knew better, though. The Bulls were no longer a one-man team. No game and no series they played would rely solely on him. He proved it, too. LA took the first game on a last-second score by Michael's old UNC teammate, Sam Perkins. But the Bulls roared back, taking the next four games in a row, and finally winning the championship.

Michael Jordan, rather than taking things into his own hands, acted throughout the series as a playmaker, demonstrating his new maturity as a player. Rather than take his own shots, he constantly played to set up his teammates. As a result, the Lakers became confused and disorganized. They didn't know who to cover. The so-called showdown between Magic and Michael never happened.

Michael Jordan scored 30 points in the last game, and had 10 assists. For the first time in 25 years, the Bulls had won the title.

"It was a seven-year struggle," Michael Jordan said. "When I first got to Chicago, we started at the bottom and every year worked harder and harder 'til we got to it. ... Now we can get rid of the stigma of the one-man team. We did it as a team all season long."

It was a great year for Michael Jordan. His achievements included being named NBA MVP for the second time, his fifth consecutive scoring title, and being named MVP of the finals. He also reached the 15,000-point level. To top it all off, perhaps the greatest prize of all for Michael Jordan was the birth of his second son, Marcus.

The Bulls charged through the 1991–92 season, finishing 67–15. There was just no way to stop the extraordinary combination of Jordan, Pippen, Paxson, and Grant. They mowed down the opposition with no apparent effort. The media began calling them "the Unbeata-Bulls."

For Michael Jordan, this amazing success meant a couple of things. For one thing, he was suddenly wealthy beyond his wildest dreams. In addition to Nike, he now had deals to represent Jeep, Quaker Oats, Gatorade, and Hanes. The income from his endorsements reached $10–15 million a year. Everywhere you turned, there were pictures of Michael Jordan on billboards, in newspapers and magazines, on TV. He had become one of the most popular figures in North America, if not the world.

But the success came with a price, and sometimes it could be a terrible price. In a way, Michael Jordan felt that he had become little more than one of the products his image was used to sell. He was no longer treated like a person. He was almost an icon, an object of almost religious worship to many.

The attention that pestered him before increased a thousand-fold. He couldn't go anywhere without attracting hordes of adoring fans clamoring for his autograph or his picture. His response was to just stay home. He became a prisoner in his own house. Mind you, his house had a nine-hole putting green in the basement, and several pool tables. But more and more, he felt like he was hiding out.

The other problem for Michael was that along with the adoring fans came the sniping critics. For every-one who wanted to put him on a pedestal and wor-ship him, there was someone else who wanted to tear him down and trample on him. The more famous he became, the louder his critics became. When the Bulls were invited to the White House to meet with President Clinton, Michael Jordan decided not to go. It was no big deal to him. He had visited the White House before, and really wanted to spend time with his family.

The media, though, threw a fit. All across the country, Michael Jordan was accused of being a spoiled superstar who didn't have to live by the same rules as his teammates. Dealing with the hurt from that was bad enough. Then the first gambling scandal broke.

Ever since he was in university, Michael Jordan had been playing golf. As with every sport he took up, he didn't do it just for fun. He loved playing, but he always played to win. The deep competitiveness of his nature showed through in everything he did. Golf was no exception. He played hard. He played to win. He believed in himself enough to put his money where his mouth was. And he had enough money to make some big bets.

Then a newspaper got hold of the story about how he lost thousands and thousands of dollars betting on golf and poker. Suddenly it was all over the news every night that Michael Jordan had a gambling problem. Nobody would even have noticed if it were some ordinary person. But because it was Michael Jordan, everybody felt they had the right to judge and condemn him. Even though the NBA investigated and determined that he had broken no rules, he was now forever stained by the accusations. They've kept coming back to haunt him over the years.

On top of all those troubles, he got a terrible phone call the winter of 1991. His friend Magic Johnson called from Los Angles to tell Michael that he was infected with HIV, the virus that causes AIDS, and was retiring from basketball. It was a terrific shock to Michael, and deeply saddened him.

Still, when the playoffs came in the spring of 1992, Michael and the rest of the Bulls were pumped and ready. The previous year they had sailed through the playoffs. This year their opponents fought them much more fiercely.

Some sports writers were ever ready to trash Michael Jordan given an opportunity. Some even suggested that the Bulls weren't hungry enough, and that they might lose to their first-round opponents, the New York Knicks.

The Knicks were an up and coming team, the same as the Bulls had been a couple of years before. They fought Chicago right down to the wire, pushing the series all the way to Game 7. But when push came to shove, Chicago pulled out the stops, trouncing the Knicks in the last game, 110–81.

They had to go another six games against Cleveland to get to the finals, where they faced the Portland Blazers. That was an incredibly hard-fought series, too. Even though Chicago ran away with the first game 122–89, Portland fought back, taking the second game 115–104 in overtime. Chicago finally won the series in six games, giving the Bulls their second NBA Championship in as many years.

That season, Michael Jordan played exceptionally well. He averaged 35.8 points per game in the Portland series. He was voted MVP of both the regular season and the finals for the second year in a row. He was the first player ever to be so honored.

"The season has been a learning experience," he told the press. Referring to the controversy and scandal that had followed him all year, he looked at the bright side. "I'm a better person for everything that has happened," he said.

Michael Jordan and hockey player Doug Gilmour enjoy a laugh at a charity golf tournament in Toronto in 1996. Golf is one of Michael's favorite sports to play during his time off.

Michael was known for sticking his tongue out as he played. Coaches over the years warned him about it, fearing he might accidently bite his tongue during a game, but apparently he never broke this habit.

Michael Jordan's number 23 was retired in 1994 when Michael left the Bulls to play baseball. When he returned to basketball in 1995, he briefly wore number 45, but soon took 23 out of retirement.

Michael scores two more points in a game against the Toronto Raptors in March 1998.

Chapter 5

The Heights and the Depths

There is no legacy. I don't have a legacy. I only have my life.
—Michael Jordan
Rebound: The Odyssey of Michael Jordan

There was no question in anyone's mind now that Michael Jordan was one of the greatest, if not *the* greatest, basketball players of all time. He had broken just about every record there was to break. He had been on two NBA championship teams, proving that he was able to lead as well as perform individually.

The one thing missing was one more NBA championship to make it three in a row. No NBA team had won three championships in a row since the Boston Celtics of the 1960s. It would the crowning achievement of Michael Jordan's extraordinary career.

But before he could get there, another matter of importance had to be dealt with first. After the Olympic Games of 1984, in which Michael Jordan had played for the US team as an amateur, the Olympic Committee had changed the rules regarding qualifications. Previously, only amateur athletes could compete in the Olympics. Now, however, because of widespread abuse of the rule by countries that paid their "amateur" athletes, the rules had been changed to allow professionals to participate as well.

As a result, the United States was fielding a team of NBA players to go to Barcelona, Spain, for the summer games in 1992. The "Dream Team," as it had been named, was to consist of the best basketball players then playing in the US. Magic Johnson came out of retirement to play. Larry Bird, Charles Barkley, and Patrick Ewing also accepted offers to play on the team. Obviously, Michael Jordan was asked as well.

Surprisingly, Michael Jordan wasn't sure he wanted to be on the team. In fact, at first he said he didn't want to play. The NBA playoffs had been grueling. He was exhausted. If he played in the Olympics it would mean giving up any time he might have with his family before the regular season started again. Besides, he had already been in the Olympics, and everybody knew this time around the "Dream Team" would rule. Nobody else stood a chance of winning against them.

There were other problems for him, too. "It was so commercialized — that was the whole point of sending us over there. It was a sales trip. We were salesmen. For the NBA," he said later. Michael Jordan saw it not so much as a sporting event as a commercial event, and as an athlete that turned him off.

But Michael remembered the bad experiences he had had with the media over the White House visit and the gambling. He was worried about what they might say about him if he turned down the offer to play on the Olympic team.

Reluctantly, he finally agreed to join the team. In a way, the issue showed how much his fame had taken over his life. Michael had no choice but to go to the Olympics, whatever he or his family wanted.

Even so, he still got in trouble. By this point in his career, he couldn't go anywhere in public without protection. Michael worried about the mobs of fans that surrounded him wherever he went. He decided to skip the opening ceremony at the Olympics. For one thing, he felt that he might personally be in some danger. But even more important, he worried that the response to him might overshadow the rest of the athletes playing in the games. That was the last thing he wanted to happen. He'd been there before in any case, and didn't feel he needed to march again.

The media didn't see it that way, and once again Michael Jordan found himself at the center of a storm. He was accused of arrogance and of snubbing the other Olympic teams.

"I was there in Barcelona, wasn't I," Michael said later. "How could I be snubbing the Olympics? I was playing in the Olympics."

The US team, as everyone expected, swept all its games. They beat Canada, Panama, Cuba, and finally Venezuela. With their 47-point victory over the Venezuelans, they took the gold medal. It was Michael Jordan's second Olympic gold medal.

The 1992–93 NBA season got off to a slow start for the Bulls. But they quickly picked up steam, and by the end of the season they finished with a 57–25 record. For the second year in a row, they never lost more than two consecutive games. Michael Jordan won his seventh straight scoring title with a 32.6 game average. It looked like they were on their way to another championship, their third in a row.

They started the playoffs strongly, too. They swept Atlanta in three games and Cleveland in four. But when they went up against the New York Knicks for the Eastern Conference Finals, they ran into trouble. The Knicks were even stronger than they'd been the year before, and some sports writers were picking them over the Bulls. Chicago lost the first game to the Knicks.

Meanwhile, the personal pressures on Michael Jordan were getting worse. He was being harassed by fans all the time. He couldn't even get away from them when he locked himself in his hotel room. The phone calls to his room were supposed to be blocked, but people still found ways to get through. They lied and said they were family, that they had medical emergencies and just had to talk to Jordan. The phone rang all the time. There was no relief for him.

Finally, his father, James Jordan, who was travelling with the Bulls, decided to get Michael away from the madness after the first game. He rented a limousine and had Michael driven to Atlantic City with a couple of friends. It was a two-hour car ride. Then Michael and his friends spent another few hours in a specially roped-off area at Bally's Casino playing blackjack before returning to New York by midnight.

It was a pretty harmless trip, except for two things. First, the next night the Bulls lost to the New York again, partly because Michael wasn't up to his usual game. Second, the press find out about his trip to Atlantic City. Putting two and two together, they accused Michael Jordan of having a gambling problem and of losing the game because he'd stayed out all night gambling. When they finally started accusing him of losing $1 million betting on golf, he'd had enough. He refused to talk to the press any longer.

He also set out to prove that he was still at the top of his game, no matter what the media said. He led the Bulls to a 103–84 victory in Game 3, and then went on to score 54 points in Game 4, leading the Bulls to another win.

After that, the Knicks seemed to have the air knocked out of them, and the Bulls went on to take the next two games and the series. They were now set up to play Phoenix in the finals.

The Phoenix Suns were not going to be a pushover. They had the best regular-season record of any team in the NBA. And they fought hard. Even after the Bulls took the first two games, Phoenix fought back and took Game 3 in triple overtime.

The Bulls weren't to be denied, however, and took Game 4, spurred on by Michael Jordan's 55-point shooting spree. The series went to six games when the Suns took Game 5.

Game 6 was played in Phoenix. It was a tough game, with both teams giving it everything they had. Phoenix knew that if they lost, it was all over. And the Bulls could see victory around the corner. Every time the Bulls pulled ahead, Phoenix would fight back.

With only seconds left in the game, the Suns were ahead 98–94. Michael Jordan closed the gap to two points. Then Scottie Pippen got the ball. He passed it to Horace Grant. Grant looked for Michael Jordan, but he was double teamed, so he threw the ball to Paxson who was in the clear behind the three-point line. Paxson shot and scored. The Bulls won, 99–98. It was their third consecutive NBA championship.

Michael Jordan was 30 years old, and was at the height of his powers. It looked like nothing could stop him. Everything he set out to win, he eventually won. There was simply no telling what he might accomplish next. It seemed as if life held out nothing but promise for Michael Jordan. Then tragedy struck.

One day in July 1993, Michael's father James left home on a short trip to visit some friends. He was supposed to be back in a couple of days. But he never showed up. The days stretched into weeks, and still there was no word from James Jordan. Everyone began to get seriously worried. They called all his friends, but no one had heard from him.

By the time Michael Jordan returned to North Carolina to be with his family, people were beginning to fear the worst. It was especially hard for Michael, who was extremely close to his father. Finally, the call they all dreaded came. James Jordan's body had been found in a creek. He had been murdered.

At first the press began to speculate that James Jordan had been killed because of Michael Jordan. People suggested that mobsters had killed him because of Michael's unpaid gambling debts. There was no truth to any of it, of course, not even any evidence. It was all pure, mean-spirited speculation, and it hurt Michael Jordan terribly.

Within days, the police arrested two 18-year-old boys. They had encountered James Jordan at a rest stop on the highway, and had robbed and killed him, in part for the NBA championship ring he wore, a gift from his son.

Michael Jordan suffered a deep crisis following his father's death. He disappeared from sight. No one heard from him for weeks. Then the Chicago Bulls called a press conference on October 6, 1993. At the conference, Michael Jordan sat in front of the microphones with his wife, Juanita, and uttered the words that shocked the world.

"I have nothing more to prove in basketball," he said. "I have no more challenges. The death of my father made me realize how short life is. I want to give more time to my family."

Michael Jordan was retiring from basketball.

Chapter 6

Starting Over

For the whole time in minor league baseball, I was reminded that if you really love playing a sport, you don't have to do it in the biggest stadiums and at the highest level.

— Michael Jordan
Rebound: The Odyssey of Michael Jordan

"You know that commercial I made for Nike about what if I was just another basketball player?" Michael Jordan once asked writer Mitchell Krugel. "'What if my face wasn't on TV every five seconds?' Well, that wasn't just done to sell shoes. That's how I really felt. There came a time when I just wanted to be another basketball player. And you know, I couldn't."

More than ever before, Michael Jordan felt trapped by his success. His father's murder affected him deeply. But it wasn't only that tragedy that led him to turn away from basketball. Over the years, he had felt the sting of media attacks. He had felt himself become more and more trapped by his fame. And perhaps most important, he had felt himself lose the feeling of joy basketball used to give him.

Michael Jordan had never been the kind of person to just let things happen to him. Quitting basketball was the first step he took toward changing his situation. Three months later he took another. Michael Jordan, the greatest basketball player of all time, announced that he was going to try out for the Chicago White Sox baseball team. He was going to try another sport and see if that way he could become just another player.

Many people couldn't believe it when Michael Jordan made the decision to play baseball professionally. They just couldn't understand why someone who was so successful in one sport would give it up to play another. They suspected his motives. Some people thought he was arrogant to assume he could go from basketball to baseball. Others thought he was just doing it for the publicity. But it turned out that Michael Jordan had been thinking about the move for some time.

"This is something my father always wanted me to do," he said. "He started me in baseball when I was six years old. Two years ago, he told me that I should go for it."

Still, thinking about it and doing it were two different things. The Bulls and the White Sox were both owned by the same people. When Michael got the idea to play baseball, he asked Jerry Reinsdorf, the owner of both teams, if he could work out with the White Sox, and got the OK.

He had been secretly working out with the team at Comiskey Park for a couple of months when he made his announcement. He knew he was a good athlete. Baseball had been his first sport. He knew he could keep up with the pros in some important skills like running. Whether he would be good enough to make the team, however, remained to be seen.

Not many people believed that Michael Jordan would seriously try to make the White Sox team. But that didn't slow him down. When spring training started in Florida in 1994, Michael Jordan reported for camp along with all the other players.

He was in for a couple of surprises, however. He had hoped the intense scrutiny of the media and his fans would end when he was just another player. And he thought he was good enough to make the team. It turned out he was wrong on both counts.

Hundreds, even thousands of fans turned out to watch Michael Jordan work out at the White Sox spring training camp. They would turn out every day to sit in the bleachers and watch for their hero. They cheered for him in the same way they always had. Nike even sent a truck full of Michael Jordan products — jerseys, hats, and shoes — to sell to the fans. Every day it parked outside the field and set up shop.

All of that would have been all right if Michael Jordan had been as good at baseball as he was at basketball. But he wasn't. He could run well. He could field a ball. But the one thing he needed to do to make the team, he couldn't do — and that was hit the ball.

Michael had his wish now. He was just another player. When he realized it wasn't all just going to fall into place for him, he responded as he had all those years ago in high school when he didn't make the varsity team. He doubled and then redoubled his effort. He worked hard at it all spring. Every day after regular practice, he got together with Walter Hriniak, the White Sox batting coach, and put in more hours.

The really terrible thing for Michael, however, wasn't discovering his weakness as a ball player. It was having to put up with the fans who continued to cheer for him even when he wasn't playing well. Every day they came and filled the stands. And every day they cheered. If he made a mediocre play, they cheered. If he dropped the ball, they cheered. When he swung the bat, they cheered whether he hit the ball or not.

It was all terrifically embarrassing for Michael Jordan. Here he was, just another player, out in the field with the other players. Some of those players were much better than he was, yet he was getting all the attention, whether he wanted it or not.

Even *Sports Illustrated* magazine got in on the act. Over the years they had named Michael Jordan athlete of the year a number of times. The last time had been just two years before. They'd used his picture on the cover to sell their magazine many times.

Now they did it again, only this time they chose to make fun of him. "Bag It, Michael! Jordan and the White Sox Are Embarrassing Baseball," the cover read. The magazine was hinting that anyone who couldn't immediately play baseball at the highest level shouldn't bother to try. It was one of the low points in *Sports Illustrated*'s history.

When the exhibition season started, the White Sox let Michael play in several exhibition games. Out of twenty at bats, he only got three hits. It quickly became clear to Michael Jordan that he wouldn't be playing with the White Sox when the regular season started.

Still, he stayed with it. He didn't expect to jump the queue. He only wanted what he could legitimately earn. He said he wanted to be just another player. Now he was. He increased the intensity of his practice, and never asked for any favors.

When the assignments were handed out at the end of spring training, Michael Jordan was assigned to a White Sox AA farm team in the Southern League — the Birmingham Barons. Michael Jordan, at 31, was the oldest player on the team. The rest were young guys in their teens and twenties hoping to work their way through the system and eventually make it to the major leagues.

Michael Jordan had already been there in basket-ball, and it was hard for his teammates to understand why someone who had achieved such success would give it up to start out at the bottom again. Most of them had grown up watching him play basketball on television. They'd seen the *Sports Illustrated* advertise-ments on TV that featured Jordan flying through the air and promised a free video of his exploits if they subscribed to the magazine. It was very strange to find themselves sharing a locker room with him. Even stranger was all the attention the team got because of his presence.

Still, he never complained about the bus rides or the bad food. He never asked for special treatment. If anything, Michael worked even harder than the rest of the team did, taking extra sessions of batting practice every day, trying to learn the basic skills he needed to succeed.

It was the same way he had mastered basketball all those years ago at Laney High School. In some ways, it felt good to him to be doing it again, even though many people laughed at him for trying. But this was the real game. This was the thing that no one could take from him or spoil — the struggle to learn, the struggle to overcome obstacles.

He actually felt good about what he was doing, despite the failures and ridicule. "This is a lot more fun than where I was last year," he said. "Last year we were trying to win a championship again for the Bulls. And we did it. If I was with the Bulls right now? We'd be trying again — but what would we be trying to do? We'd be trying to duplicate — duplicate something we'd already accomplished. There's nothing in that for me."

And he was right in the middle of the romance of baseball. He was back where all that mattered was playing. But like basketball, baseball was changing. It wasn't just a game any more, it was big business. And the business side of major league baseball was just about to take over. Within a few months the major league players would go on strike. There would be no baseball season, no World Series. Fans would have to wait while the millionaire owners and the millionaire players fought over the division of the spoils.

But standing out in right field in some little ballpark in some little town in the American South, the only thing that mattered was the game itself and how well you could play. It was the same game that young people had been thrilled to play for over a hundred years in sandlots and tiny fields all over North and South America. It was baseball. And Michael Jordan was playing. He was just another player. That was all that mattered.

"I liked the work," Michael Jordan said later, looking back on his baseball experience. "I liked going out there and taking all that batting practice. I liked taking nothing about my game for granted. I liked the feeling that I could never assume that I could succeed."

And it looked for a while like the work was paying off. When the season opened for the Barons, Michael Jordan started off batting well. He had a 13-game hitting streak, and when it ended was batting .378. But it did end, and it wasn't long before his average fell drastically, to around .200. That's where it stayed for much of the rest of the season.

It was depressing for Jordan. He did everything he could to bring his batting up to snuff, but nothing seemed to work for him. He even dropped down to .193 at one point. But he never thought about quitting.

Finally, at the end of July, he got his first home run. That seemed to turn things around for him, and he started connecting with the ball again. By the end of August he was batting .260, good enough to raise his overall season average to .202. He also hit three home runs, had fifty-one RBIs, and led the league in stolen bases with thirty. All in all, not bad for a basketball player. He felt that things were beginning to come together for him, and that next year he might make the majors after all.

Meanwhile things were changing in Chicago. For one thing, the Bulls didn't win the NBA championship for the fourth year in a row. They didn't do badly, however. They had an overall 55–27 record and made it all the way to the Eastern Conference semi-finals. This time, though, they couldn't get past the Knicks, and went down in seven games.

Michael Jordan's fabulous feats on the basketball court had drawn many new fans to the Chicago Bulls games. To accommodate them, the Bulls management had decided to tear down the old Chicago Stadium and build a new super sports complex, the United Center. That fall, Scottie Pippen organized a charity game to say goodbye to the old stadium. He asked Michael Jordan to play, and Michael agreed.

There was tremendous excitement over the return of Jordan to Chicago. The building was packed the night of the game. He didn't disappoint. He scored 52 points, more than any player on either team. As the game was ending and he was leaving the court, Michael Jordan got down on his hands and knees and kissed the painted Bull in the middle of the floor. Many fans were weeping as he walked off the court for the last time.

That fall, Michael Jordan got permission to play in the Arizona Fall League, in order to keep working on his baseball skills. He briefly flew back to Chicago when the Bulls retired his old number, 23. Then he got back to the business of working on his baseball game.

His hitting was getting much better. Many people agreed that he was beginning to look like a real ball player. Not, perhaps, a great ball player. Not yet anyway. But at least an ordinary ball player, which was progress. He was learning the game. He was hanging in. What he needed was more time. But as it turned out, that's the one thing he didn't have.

What finally stopped him was the major league player strike of 1994–95. They'd been out since August, and as spring training approached, the owners announced that they were going to field teams of replacement players in order to get the season going.

Michael had a deal with Jerry Reinsdorf that he wouldn't be asked to be a replacement player. The last thing he wanted was to make it to the major leagues that way. He could see the headlines, and they wouldn't be pretty. Even more important, whatever he thought of the strike, he couldn't stab his fellow athletes in the back.

"I had told them from the beginning that I didn't want them to use my name to make money in the spring training games," he said later. "We had an understanding. It was never even supposed to come up."

But it did come up.

Michael Jordan reported for spring training in February. As the exhibition season opened, the White Sox management decided that any minor leaguers who refused to play in White Sox uniforms would be forbidden access to the main clubhouse. More and more pressure was put on Jordan to suit up and play as a replacement player. Finally, in disgust, he left spring training. Clearly, now he would never play baseball for Chicago.

Michael Jordan's career as a baseball player was over.

Chapter 7

Back for More

Even if they don't say it out loud, I know there are times
when they look at me on the court and think: Who's he? Like
what am I doing here and what do I want? They have a
right to think that. I'm the one who left and came back.

— Michael Jordan
Rebound: The Odyssey of Michael Jordan

On March 8, 1995, the Chicago Bulls released to the media a statement from Michael Jordan. It was short and to the point: "I'm back," it said. Michael Jordan was returning to the Chicago Bulls in mid-season. It immediately became the biggest news story of the day.

Jordan was returning to a vastly different team from the one he had left a year and a half before. The "threepeat" championship team of the early '90s that had taken six years of patient work to build was no more. John Paxson had left to become a broadcaster. Horace Grant had become a free agent. No longer bound to Chicago, Grant had negotiated a contract with Orlando. The team that was left had only a .500

record when Jordan came back, with 34 wins and 32 losses.

Michael Jordan was in a difficult position. Baseball demanded a different kind of fitness than basketball. He was more out of shape for basketball than he'd ever been. He was also older. Those fans who expected to see the Michael Jordan of old — the leaping, flying, shooting whirlwind — were bound to be disappointed. It didn't help that his first game back the Bulls lost to Indiana, 103–96. People began to wonder out loud if he should have come back at all.

But Michael Jordan wasn't about to give up. He had only just started again. As he worked at his game, improving his own skills and learning how to work with the new Bulls, the team began to get stronger. The Bulls went 13–4 in the last 17 games of the season, finishing in third place in the central division. Michael Jordan averaged 26.9 points in those last games. Not bad for someone who had been away from the game as long as he had.

In the first round of the playoffs, the Bulls beat the Charlotte Hornets in four games. Michael was up to his old tricks again, including a left-handed, floating reverse underhand flip layup off the glass. As a team, though, the Bulls still weren't functioning up to speed. When it came to the second round of the playoffs against the Orlando Magic, it showed.

With Michael's old teammate, Horace Grant, now playing inside for the Magic, the Bulls found the going tough. The Orlando Magic also had Shaquille O'Neal, now billed as "the new Michael Jordan."

The first game didn't go well at all for the Bulls. They had the game all but won, which would have meant getting the home court advantage from Orlando. Then Michael Jordan blew it.

The Bulls were ahead 91–90 with 18 seconds left when Jordan lost the ball to Anfernee Hardaway. Hardaway passed to Grant under the net and Grant scored. Then Jordan got the ball again, but threw it away in a bad pass to Scottie Pippen.

"I feel personally responsible," Jordan told reporters after the game.

Because Chicago had retired Jordan's old number, 23, he was now wearing his baseball number, 45. After the game, the Magic's Nick Anderson told the media, "Number 45 doesn't explode like number 23. Number 23, he could blow by you. He took off like a space shuttle. Number 45 revs up, but he doesn't really take off."

If Anderson was out to get Jordan's goat, he succeeded, in spades. Jordan was furious. When he came out on the court at the beginning of Game 2, he had a surprise for Nick Anderson and the rest of the world. He was wearing his old number, 23. This caused a huge controversy, because he never bothered to ask permission from the NBA to take the number out of retirement.

But that would have taken time and Michael Jordan wanted to make a point now, whatever it might cost him in fines for breaking the rules. If anybody had any lingering questions, he put them to rest. He dominated the game, scoring 38 points and leading Chicago to a 104-94 victory.

But finally, that kind of individual effort wasn't enough to overcome the teamwork of the Magic. Orlando and Chicago traded wins in Games 3 and 4, but then Orlando took the next two, knocking Chicago out of the competition.

Even though they were out of the running for the championship for that year, the Bulls still had high hopes for the 1995–96 season. After all, Michael Jordan was back.

For the entire off-season, Michael Jordan had to listen to the pundits and armchair athletes rattle on and on about how he wasn't the same player, how he had lost his edge, how he was getting old. Michael Jordan responded as he always did in such circumstances — he worked harder, pushing himself to the limit, and then a little beyond.

Thinking about his baseball experience, he said, "The one thing I know is that I like the stairs. That's where I'm at my best — climbing the stairs. I'd forgotten that, and baseball gave it back to me. It let me find out what the stairs felt like again. The stairs feel good. They're where I belong."

The first thing he did that summer was make a movie. The Walt Disney Corporation had made him a standing offer couple of years before to star in a movie with animated characters. That year he took them up on it. The result was the hit movie, *Space Jam.*

He also spent the summer getting back in shape. The Bulls made an important change, too, acquiring Dennis Rodman from the Detroit Pistons to fill in for the missing Horace Grant under the net.

The rest, as they say, is history.

Those who thought Michael Jordan was finished were in for a shock. It was "Threepeat" all over again as the Bulls went on to win NBA championships in 1996, 1997, and 1998. And it was Michael Jordan who led them.

Jordan continued to wear number 23. He also continued to break records. By the end of the 1998 season and the Bulls' hard-won championship victory over the Utah Jazz, Jordan had collected ten scoring titles, five season MVPs, and six finals MVPs.

But things could not go on the same forever. At the end of the '98 season, the future was unclear. Coach Phil Jackson was fired from his job. Jackson was later offered his job back, but he turned it down. He said he had some disagreements with people in the Bulls management.

That was bad news for the Bulls, because Michael Jordan had stated publicly that he would only play for Jackson.

On top of that came news of a breakdown in negotiations between the players and the owners. The two groups could not agree on the terms for their contracts. The team owners ended up "locking out" the players. A "lockout" is something like a strike. In a strike, employees refuse to work. In a lockout the employers don't allow the employees to work until they agree on their contract. This lockout delayed the opening of the 1998–99 NBA season until early January of 1999.

Almost as soon as the end of the lockout was announced, people began to wonder what Michael Jordan would do. He would turn 36 in February. Most professional basketball players retire around that age. Would Michael ever return to the courts?

The suspense ended on January 13, 1999, when Michael Jordan and his wife Juanita appeared at a press conference in Chicago. There Michael announced his second retirement from professional basketball. He said he was "99.9 percent" sure his retirement would be permanent this time.

"I played it to the best I could play it," Michael said. "I tried to be the best basketball player I could be. ... This is a perfect time for me to walk away from the game. I'm at peace with that."

Bulls chairman Jerry Reinsdorf was also at the press conference. He said, "Michael is simply the best player who ever put on a basketball uniform."

After Michael's announcement, the president of the United States, Bill Clinton, said Jordan had "a remarkable set of qualities of mind, body and spirit ... who always expected to do whatever it was he tried to do."

No one can say for sure what's next for Michael Jordan. He has led an exciting life, a life full of joy and achievement, and sometimes terrific sadness. He has always pushed himself. He has never been afraid to take chances, even when many people scoffed at him. Through great effort and courage he has taken his natural skills and used them to reach heights most people only dream of.

Whatever else people may think of Michael Jordan, everyone has to agree on one thing:

He has soared.

Glossary of Basketball Terms

assist — a pass that results directly in a basket

basket — the hoop through which the ball is thrown; to successfully throw the ball through the hoop (to make a basket)

bounce pass — a pass thrown from one teammate to another, usually on one bounce

center — usually the team's tallest player, who patrols the area near the basket

charging — a personal foul, committed when a player with the ball charges into an opponent who has established defensive position

double team — to use two defensive players to cover one offensive player. Also triple team and quadruple team.

dunk — to put the ball into the basket from above the rim

fast break — to run downcourt quickly, before the opposing team has an opportunity to organize its defense

foul — illegal contact, by either a defensive player or an offensive player

foul shot or free throw — an unhindered shot, worth one point, from the foul line or freethrow line by a player who has been fouled

fullcourt press — a defensive tactic in which each player covers an opposing player closely all over the court, even before the opposing team has put the ball into play

hook shot — a high-arcing shot taken, usually by a center, using a sweeping motion with the player's back to the basket after pivoting on the foot opposite to the shooting hand

jump shot — a shot taken after a player has jumped straight up in the air

layup — a shot, usually banked off the backboard, taken from the side of the basket or from in front of the basket

lane — the area inside the two parallel lines that extend from the foul line or freethrow line to the baseline at each end of the court

open man — a player without the ball who is in a good position to shoot

pivotman — a player positioned near the basket who takes a pass, then either pivots to either side while taking a hook shot or throws the ball back to a teammate

point guard — a backcourt player who brings the ball upcourt, then controls the offense by starting a set play or by throwing a pass to the open man

power forward — a frontcourt player, usually the team's best rebounder

rebound — to grab the ball off either the offensive backboard or the defensive backboard

screen — a play set when an offensive player establishes position in front of a defensive player, thereby enabling a teammate to get free for a shot or a drive to the basket

shooting guard — a backcourt player whose primary role is to shoot rather than to set up plays

steal — to take the ball away from an offensive player without committing a foul

three point line — the line around the key, outside of which a basket is worth three points. Inside the line, baskets are worth two points

zone defense — when the defensive players are assigned a specific area (or zone) of the court to cover, rather than being assigned to a particular offensive player

Research Sources

"Being Michael Jordan," *Vanity Fair* , October, 1998: 118–119.

Christopher, Matt. *On the Court with . . . Michael Jordan.* Boston: Little Brown and Co., 1996.

Greene, Bob. *Rebound: The Odyssey of Michael Jordan.* New York: Signet, 1995.

Krugel, Mitchell. *Jordan: The Man, His Words, His Life.* New York: St. Martin's, 1998.

Lovitt, Chip. *Michael Jordan.* New York: Scholastic, 1993.